Analytical Thinking

An Overview Based on Data Decision-Making

Epris E. Ezekiel

Copyright 2024© Epris E. Ezekiel
All rights reserved. This book is copyrighted and no part of it may be reproduced, distributed, or transmitted in any form or by any means, including photocopying, recording, or other electronic or mechanical methods, without the prior written permission of the publisher, except in the case of brief quotations embodied in critical reviews and certain other non-commercial uses permitted by copyright law.
Printed in the United States of America
Copyright 2024© Epris E. Ezekiel

Contents

Introduction 1

Chapter 1 2

What is analytical thinking? 2

Chapter 2 7

Practical Applications of Analytical Thinking 7

Chapter 3 16

How Do You Master Analytical Thinking? 16

Chapter 4 22

Who Can Benefit from Analytical Thinking? 22

Chapter 5 28

Making data-driven decisions? 28

Chapter 6 36

Challenges of DDDM 36

Chapter 7 44

Bias in data and algorithms 44

Conclusion 56

Introduction

Are you wondering how to improve your problem-solving abilities and make better-informed decisions? Understanding what Analytical Thinking is will help you unleash these abilities. Analytical thinking entails breaking down complex material into smaller, more digestible chunks, allowing you to identify patterns and develop significant conclusions.

In this article, we will shed light on the fundamental concepts of analytical thinking and demonstrate its significance in both personal and professional settings. By the conclusion, you'll understand what Analytical Thinking is and how you can use it to improve your decision-making. Discover the revolutionary power of analytical thinking today!

Chapter 1

What is analytical thinking?

Analytical thinking is the cognitive process of breaking down complex problems, data sets, or situations into smaller, more manageable chunks to discover patterns, linkages, and fundamental principles. It entails careful observation, logical thinking, and systematic analysis to reach well-informed findings or answers. This skill enables people to make informed judgments, promote creativity, and effectively express complex ideas.

Analytical Thinking is the foundation of effective problem-solving, enabling people to face issues with accuracy and adaptability, whether in everyday life, business, or academia. Honing this skill allows one to confidently negotiate difficulties, resulting in more strategic and perceptive outcomes.

Key Aspects of Analytical Thinking

Analytical Thinking includes numerous significant subtopics that contribute to an individual's expertise in this important skill:

Mastering Analytical Thinking

Analytical Thinking is a complicated skill that involves both information and practice. Individuals can master Analytical Thinking by honing their skills in data evaluation and interpretation, pattern recognition, problem decomposition, critical analysis, logical reasoning, and creative problem-solving. Emphasizing these critical components in assessments and developing these talents within your business will help Analytical Thinking reach its full potential, resulting in better strategic decision-making, inventive problem-solving, and overall success.

Creativity in Problem Solving

While Analytical Thinking is generally associated with logical and methodical analysis, it also includes an element of creativity. Skilled Analytical Thinkers can combine their excellent analytical ability with creative thinking to come up with novel solutions and approaches to issues. This combination of creative and analytical abilities gives a distinct and valuable dimension to problem-solving procedures.

Logical reasoning and deductive thought

Logical reasoning is an important aspect of analytical thinking. Individuals with this competence can use deductive or inductive reasoning to reach logical conclusions from existing information. Analytical thinkers use logical thinking processes to connect pieces of information, examine cause-and-effect relationships, and produce cohesive and rational answers.

Critical Analysis and Evaluation

Analytical thinkers are naturally drawn to critical analysis. They can objectively evaluate information, arguments, and ideas, balancing the advantages and disadvantages of various viewpoints. Individuals can make the most rational and informed decisions by thoroughly assessing available options and prospective solutions.

Problem Decomposition and Root Cause Analysis.

Analytical thinkers can break down big situations into smaller, more manageable components. They thoroughly study each component, attempting to grasp the underlying causes and elements that contribute to the problem. Individuals can undertake detailed root-cause analyses to address fundamental problems and generate focused solutions, resulting in more effective problem-solving.

Pattern Recognition and Analysis

Pattern recognition is an essential component of analytical thinking. Individuals with this competence may discover underlying patterns, correlations, and trends in complex data sets. Analytical Thinkers can build effective strategies or solutions by detecting repeating themes or linkages.

Data analysis and interpretation

Analytical thinkers are skilled in analyzing and interpreting facts to draw relevant insights. They have a good sense of detail and can assess the quality, dependability, and significance of data. Individuals can extract important information, spot trends, and make educated decisions by scrutinizing databases and using their analytical skills.

Chapter 2

Practical Applications of Analytical Thinking

Analytical thinking is a skill that may be applied in a variety of fields and industries. Its methodical and logical approach to issue-solving makes it extremely adaptable and useful in a variety of professional situations. Here are a few practical examples of analytical thinking:

Scientific Research and Experimentation

Analytical thinking is the foundation of scientific study and experimentation. Scientists use this competence to design experiments, examine data, generate hypotheses, and reach conclusions. Scientists can use Analytical Thinking to ensure the validity and dependability of their study, thereby contributing to the growth of knowledge in their domains.

Incorporating Analytical Thinking into

organizational frameworks across these disciplines and beyond allows professionals to improve problem-solving skills, make data-driven decisions, stimulate innovation, and succeed in a quickly changing environment.

Financial analysis and forecasting

Analytical Thinking is essential for financial analysis and forecasting. Financial workers use Analytical Thinking skills to examine financial data, recognize trends, forecast future performance, and make financial decisions. They provide significant insights that help businesses expand and stabilize by examining financial statements, market situations, and economic indicators.

Scientific Research and Experimentation
Analytical thinking is the foundation of scientific study and experimentation. Scientists use this competence to design experiments, examine data, generate hypotheses, and reach conclusions. Scientists can use Analytical Thinking to ensure the validity and dependability of their study, thereby contributing to the growth of knowledge in their domains.

Incorporating Analytical Thinking into organizational frameworks across these disciplines and beyond allows professionals to improve problem-solving skills, make data-driven decisions, stimulate innovation, and succeed in a quickly changing environment.

Innovation and Process Improvement. Analytical thinking promotes creativity and process improvement. Professionals with Analytical Thinking skills can lead innovation projects by examining existing processes, finding bottlenecks, and discovering potential for optimization. They can suggest and implement changes, streamline operations, and boost organizational efficiency.

Risk Assessment and Management

Analytical thinking is useful in analyzing and controlling hazards. Individuals with Analytical Thinking skills can thoroughly assess potential hazards, examine risk variables, and estimate the likelihood and significance of various outcomes. This allows firms to make educated decisions, reduce risks, and successfully manage difficult situations.

Problem Solving and Troubleshooting

Analytical thinking is essential while solving problems. Analytical Thinkers use their abilities to break down problems, evaluate information, and discover core causes to handle operational inefficiencies, customer difficulties, and complicated obstacles. This competence allows them to create targeted solutions and implement effective tactics.

Business Strategy and Decision-making

Organizational strategic planning and decision-making rely heavily on analytical thinking. By critically examining market trends, competition data, and internal performance measures, Analytical Thinking experts may find opportunities, analyze risks, and make educated decisions that correspond with company goals and create success.

Research and Data Analysis

Analytical thinking is critical in research and data analysis projects. Professionals with this competence can efficiently collect, evaluate, and interpret data to discover insights, patterns, and trends. Analytical Thinking enables researchers to perform complete investigations, reach correct conclusions, and provide data-driven suggestions.

Why Is Analytical Thinking Important?
After learning about Analytical Thinking, let's look at its multidimensional importance:

1. **Continuous Improvement.**

    Analytical thinkers have a natural curiosity that drives them to continually study and progress. They see setbacks as opportunities to progress rather than insurmountable hurdles. This commitment to self-improvement extends beyond their abilities; analytical thinkers frequently attempt to enhance procedures, systems, and products, contributing to progress in their domains and businesses.

2. **Critical Evaluation**

    In today's world of misinformation and biased narratives, critical thinking skills are more important than ever. Analytical thinking enables people to filter through large amounts of information, find reputable sources, and discriminate between reality and fiction. This discriminating skill guards against being duped by surface allure or false claims.

3. **Strategic Planning**

    Strategic planning, whether for corporate or personal goals, requires the capacity to predict outcomes, develop contingencies, and react to changing conditions. Analytical thinking helps individuals develop strategic acumen by allowing them to examine many variables, anticipate potential hurdles, and create a course that maximizes the likelihood of success.

4. **precise communication**

   Clear and effective communication is essential in every part of life. Analytical thinking improves the capacity to arrange thoughts logically, build arguments clearly, and communicate ideas precisely. Whether expressing a topic to a colleague, making a persuasive pitch, or writing a research paper, an analytical thinker's ability to articulate complicated ideas clearly and comprehensibly is priceless.

5. **Innovative problem-solving**

   The capacity to connect seemingly unconnected concepts and unearth hidden solutions is frequently what drives innovation. Analytical thinkers are adept at breaking down complex situations into manageable components and reassembling them in creative ways. This cognitive flexibility promotes innovation by allowing people to see alternate paths and techniques that would otherwise be hidden.

6. **Informed Decision-making**

At its foundation, Analytical Thinking equips people with the capacity to examine complex events, retrieve pertinent information, and make sound decisions. Whether you're considering a career shift, analyzing a large investment, or deciding on the best course of action, Analytical Thinking allows you to weigh the pros and disadvantages, detect potential hazards, and accurately predict results.

Chapter 3

How Do You Master Analytical Thinking?

To improve your Analytical Thinking abilities, you can apply the following skills:

1. Organizing information requires carefully arranging and integrating all acquired data to gain insights and produce ideas, setting the framework for potential solutions to the challenges at hand.

2. Identifying the root cause entails undertaking a thorough investigation to discover the underlying cause of a problem, ensuring that efforts are directed toward fixing the actual issue rather than merely its symptoms.

3. Identifying difficulties and problems entails improving the ability to recognize underlying issues or challenges by studying trends, associations, and cause-and-effect linkages within datasets.

4. Gathering information is asking essential questions of oneself and others to gather significant insights and facilitate more informed decision-making while addressing difficulties.

5. Breaking down difficulties reduces larger challenges by breaking them into smaller, more manageable concerns that may be solved individually.

6. Analyzing information is thoroughly evaluating facts or a situation to find critical parts, assessing their strengths

and weaknesses, and using this knowledge to build a compelling argument, make recommendations, or successfully handle a problem.

Roles that require strong analytical thinking skills

Analytical thinking is a valuable skill in a variety of occupations. Here are some roles that require somebody with good analytical thinking skills:

1. **Supply Analysts:** Supply Analysts use Analytical Thinking to analyze supply chain data, estimate demand, and optimize inventory management to improve operational efficiency.

2. **Machine Learning Engineer:** Machine Learning Engineers use Analytical Thinking to create and optimize machine learning models, analyze data, and design

algorithms to solve complicated problems.

3. **Front-End Developer:** Front-End Developers utilize Analytical Thinking to plan and build user-friendly interfaces, resulting in optimal user experiences through data-driven design decisions.

4. **Data Pipeline Engineer:** Data Pipeline Engineers use Analytical Thinking to design, implement, and maintain efficient data pipelines and workflows, allowing data to flow seamlessly between systems.

5. **Data Governance Analysts:** Data Governance Analysts use Analytical Thinking to develop and implement data governance rules and processes, assuring data quality and compliance within businesses.

6. **Analytics Engineers:** Analytic Engineers use Analytical Thinking to create and manage data analysis infrastructure, allowing firms to extract insights and make sound business decisions.

7. **Product Analysts:** Product Analysts employ Analytical Thinking to assess user data, conduct market research, and find chances for product enhancement, all of which contribute to the creation of successful products.

8. **Marketing Analysts:** Marketing Analysts use Analytical Thinking to assess market trends, customer behavior, and campaign success to effectively optimize marketing strategies and promote business growth.

9. **Insights Analyst:** Insights Analysts use Analytical Thinking to study data, discover relevant trends, and provide actionable insights to help businesses plan and make decisions.
10. **Data Engineers:** Data engineers use Analytical Thinking to design, create, and optimize data pipelines and infrastructure, ensuring that data is stored and processed efficiently.
11. **Data Scientists:** Data Scientists use Analytical Thinking to extract knowledge and patterns from massive datasets, then use statistical analysis and machine learning approaches to solve complicated issues.
12. **Data Analysts:** Data Analysts use Analytical Thinking to collect, analyze, and understand large amounts of data, resulting in significant insights that drive company choices and strategies.

Chapter 4

Who Can Benefit from Analytical Thinking?

Analytical thinking is extremely advantageous to professionals in a variety of disciplines, particularly those that require strong problem-solving and decision-making skills.

1. **Freelancers:** Freelancers gain from better project management, making educated decisions, and adjusting to changing client needs, which increases overall productivity and client satisfaction.

2. **CEOs:** CEOs rely on analytical thinking to make strategic decisions, drive business growth, and navigate difficult market settings, all of which contribute to long-term success.

3. **Software engineers:** Analytical thinking enables software developers to enhance code efficiency, diagnose complicated problems, and create more resilient and efficient software solutions.

4. **Designers:** Designers can improve their problem-solving skills and creativity by using analytical thinking, resulting in more original and user-centric solutions.

How do you apply analytical thinking to management and decision-making?

Analytical thinking is a method of thinking that emphasizes facts, evidence, and reasoning. It is used to solve problems and make decisions by logically reviewing and processing data to choose the optimal approach.

Here's how you can apply analytical thinking in your life and at work:

- ❖ **Identify the problem.**

Analytical thinkers are adept at identifying their difficulties. They pose queries such as "What is the problem?" or "What is the situation?" Once they've discovered the problem, they divide it into smaller pieces to better understand it. This simplifies the issue and makes finding answers to complex problems much easier.

- ❖ **Consider possible solutions and analyze them.**

    Once you have a comprehensive understanding of your problem and its causes, consider potential solutions. Analytical thinkers take their time weighing all options before concluding. They consider not only what is desirable, but also what is realistic given their resources and other restraints. They ask themselves questions such as "How do I solve this?", "How much will this cost?", "How long will it take?", and "Is there another way?"

- ❖ **Obtain the appropriate training and skills.**

  Being intuitive isn't enough to build effective analytical thinking skills. You must receive proper training to learn about the various parts and disciplines of analytical thinking, as well as how to use them in your company. Data analysis training is an excellent approach to guarantee that you have the necessary abilities and understand how to use them effectively.

- ❖ **Develop hypotheses.**

After defining the problem, explore several analytic hypotheses about how it could be solved or avoided in the future. For example, if your company has been losing clients owing to high shipping costs or late deliveries, one hypothesis might be that giving free overnight delivery will help win back their business; another could be that cutting pricing would assist increase sales volume.

❖ Assess each idea's potential impact and chances of success.

For example, if you want to establish an online business selling things but have never sold anything online before, analyzing your alternatives based on prospective impact may entail comparing how much money you could make from this type of business to other options.

❖ Gather all essential data.

This step involves any previous study or analysis, as well as any fresh data or ideas required to solve the problem or achieve your goal. Statistical understanding and problem-solving are two important data analysis abilities to acquire if you want to improve your analytical thinking. Having these abilities ensures that your decisions are data-driven and reasonable.

Chapter 5

Making data-driven decisions?

Data-driven decision-making (DDDM) is defined as the use of facts, measurements, and data to influence strategic business decisions that are consistent with your goals, objectives, and initiatives. When organizations see the full value of their data, everyone—whether a business analyst, sales manager, or human resource specialist—is empowered to make better data-driven decisions daily. However, this is not accomplished simply by selecting the appropriate analytical tool to uncover the next strategic opportunity. Your firm must establish data-driven decision-making as the standard, fostering a culture of critical thinking and inquiry. People at all levels engage in data-driven conversations, and they improve their data abilities via practice and application.

Fundamentally, this necessitates a self-service architecture in which users can access the data they desire while maintaining security and oversight. It also necessitates training and development opportunities for employees to master data skills. Finally, executive advocacy and a community that supports and makes data-driven decisions will inspire others to follow suit.

Establishing these key competencies would foster data-driven decision-making at all levels, allowing business units to frequently query and investigate information to uncover compelling insights that drive action.

Steps for making excellent data-driven decisions

These steps will assist you in determining the "who, what, where, when, and why" of data to maximize its value for you, your colleagues, and the organization. However, keep in mind that the cycle of visual analysis is not linear. One question frequently leads to another, which may require you to return to one of these steps or jump to the next, ultimately leading to useful discoveries.

1. **Identify business objectives:** This phase requires an awareness of your organization's executive and downstream goals. This could be as concrete as increasing sales and website traffic, or as nebulous as raising brand awareness. This will assist you later in the process in selecting key performance indicators (KPIs) and metrics that influence data-driven decisions, as well as determining which data to analyze and what questions to ask so that your analysis supports key business objectives. For example, if a marketing effort is aimed at increasing website traffic, a KPI could be linked to the number of contact submissions

received so that sales can follow up with leads.

2. **Survey business teams to find critical data sources:** To achieve success, it is critical to solicit input from people within the business to comprehend short and long-term objectives. These inputs help to shape the questions people ask in their analyses, as well as how you prioritize authorized data sources.

Valuable inputs from throughout the organization will help to drive your analytics deployment and future state, including roles, responsibilities, architecture, and processes, as well as success metrics to track progress.

3. **Collect and prepare the information you require:** Accessing excellent, trustworthy data can be difficult if your company's information is spread across multiple unrelated sources. You can begin data preparation once you understand the extent of your organization's data sources.

   Begin by preparing data sources with high impact and low complexity. Prioritize data sources with the largest audiences so that you may have an instant impact. Start by using these resources to create a high-impact dashboard.

4. **View and examine data:** Visualizing your data is critical for DDDM. Representing your thoughts in a visually impactful manner increases your chances of influencing senior leadership and other employees' actions.

Data visualization, which uses various visual components such as charts, graphs, and maps, is an easy way to observe and analyze trends, outliers, and patterns in data. There are numerous popular visualization types for successfully displaying information, including a bar chart for comparison, a map for spatial data, a line chart for temporal data, and a scatter plot to compare two metrics, among others.

5. **Develop insights:** Critical thinking with data entails discovering insights and articulating them in a meaningful, engaging manner. Visual analytics is a simple method for asking and answering questions about your data. Discover opportunities or hazards that may affect success or issue solutions.

JPMorgan Chase adopted a sophisticated analytics system to make critical decisions for the bank's health. JPMC obtains a holistic perspective of the customer journey by combining line-of-business relationships (i.e. product, marketing, and service contact points) with customer data. For example, the Marketing Operations team conducts analyses that affect design decisions for the website, advertising materials, and products such as the Chase mobile app.

6. **Act on and share your insights:** Once you've discovered an insight, you should act on it or share it with others to collaborate. One method to accomplish this is to share dashboards. Highlighting crucial insights through informative text and interactive visualizations can

influence your audience's decisions and help them take more educated actions in their everyday work.

Data-Driven Decision Making: Benefits and Challenges

Data-driven decision-making (DDDM) has acquired significant popularity in the business sector in recent years. It is a process in which organizational leaders and decision-makers use facts to guide their decisions rather than depending primarily on intuition or experience. This technique enables firms to generate more accurate predictions, increase efficiency, and, ultimately, drive growth. However, as with every strategic endeavor, DDDM presents its own set of problems and opportunities. To fully use this method for organizational success, it's critical to comprehend both sides of the coin: the potential drawbacks and the tremendous benefits.

Chapter 6

Challenges of DDDM

Data-driven decision-making (DDDM) is an extremely useful tool for enterprises. However, it is not without its obstacles. To effectively use data in decision-making, companies must first overcome various roadblocks that can impede its implementation.

One of the major challenges is managing huge data. 90% of the world's data has been created in the last two years. This tremendous influx of information creates new challenges for leaders and decision-makers attempting to extract valuable insights from their data sets. Another major problem is ensuring that all team members understand and appreciate the DDDM principles. Even well-intentioned attempts can fail if they lack universal buy-in and comprehension.

In the following sections, we'll look at these challenges in greater detail, as well as other potential DDDM pitfalls such as data quality concerns, privacy risks, integration headaches, and so on. Recognizing these problems head-on can better prepare your organization to navigate them successfully.

Integration of Data from Different Sources

Data-driven decision-making frequently necessitates gathering information from a range of sources. This approach might be fairly difficult for organizations. Why? Data comes in many formats and structures depending on where it came from.

For example, you might receive client feedback via social media comments, email surveys, or direct interviews. Each of these sites delivers useful information, but they present it in various ways.

This is where the idea of data integration comes into play. It is about bringing together this disparate set of facts into a uniform view that decision-makers inside an organization can easily assess and understand.

However, attaining successful integration is not always easy. There may be compatibility difficulties between different types of datasets that must be addressed before they may function together seamlessly.

Furthermore, combining enormous amounts of complicated data without losing crucial details is another challenge to tackle. However, with strong tactics and current technologies built expressly for this goal, such as specialist software or platforms, these obstacles become more doable.

So, while combining diverse types of data sources may create some initial challenges when done correctly, it becomes a strong tool that dramatically improves your data analytics capabilities.

Data Quality and Integrity.

Data quality and integrity are critical factors in data-driven decision-making. The correctness of the decisions is strongly dependent on the quality of the data used. For example, making judgments based on faulty or outdated information can result in misdirected strategies that can harm your organization.

Organizations frequently face the challenge of coping with incomplete data collection. If some bits of information are missing from your database, it may distort your analysis and lead to incorrect results. Similarly, inaccurate data submissions can distort the big picture and mislead decision-makers.

Poor data quality is the most significant obstacle that 43% of firms face when using DDDM methods. This underscores the need to keep high-quality datasets for successful decision-making.

Furthermore, ensuring that team members have an analytical mindset helps to sustain this focus on quality throughout all stages, from gathering raw data to evaluating outcomes, so improving both integrity and reliability in our decision-making process. Remember that, while using large amounts of big data can be useful for gaining insights into trends or patterns within an organization's operations, these efforts may backfire if proper quality control measures are not followed, leading us down the wrong paths rather than guiding us toward success.

Data Privacy and Security Concerns

Data privacy is a significant consideration when implementing data-driven decision-making. Organizations are responsible for protecting huge amounts of data from unlawful access or misuse.

Data breaches provide a substantial danger. A single breach can cause significant financial losses, harm your brand, and lose customer trust. As a result, robust security measures are no longer an option, but a requirement in today's business climate.

Transparency is another important component of data privacy. Our organization must be transparent about how we acquire and handle the data given to us by our customers or clients. This transparency promotes stakeholder trust while also assuring compliance with various data usage requirements.

Finally, resolving these security and privacy problems is critical to the successful implementation of any approach that relies on large amounts of collected data for decision-making.

Overcoming Data Illiteracy.

Data literacy refers to the capacity to read, comprehend, and communicate data as information. Data literacy has become a vital ability in the business sector, much as literacy in reading and writing is for daily chores. However, not everyone in an organization may possess this skill set. Organizations must understand that their decision-making process is only as good as the individuals who interpret the facts. This means that managers must be knowledgeable about data and how to use it efficiently.

Continuous education and training initiatives are one way for an organization to improve its data literacy. These programs can assist employees to get more familiar with numbers and understand how to read them effectively.

Another technique could be to cultivate a data-driven culture in which decisions are made using real information rather than intuition or gut impressions. Employees in such situations are encouraged to use data frequently, which gradually increases their comfort with it.

In essence, overcoming data illiteracy requires investing time in educating your team about what constitutes relevant metrics or key performance indicators (KPIs), how they're measured, and why they matter for your specific business objectives - essentially, ensuring that everyone understands how their role fits into the larger picture of being a truly 'data-driven' company.

Chapter 7

Bias in data and algorithms

Bias is a component that can enter into data sets and algorithms, frequently without our knowledge. It's like an unwelcome guest at a party: you didn't invite it, but it somehow made its way in. When prejudice infiltrates our data or the algorithms, we employ to evaluate it, it can skew the results and lead to decisions based on incorrect information.

For example, if your organization only collects customer feedback via online surveys, you may be losing out on opinions from customers who prefer alternative communication channels or do not have internet access. This generates a bias toward the opinions of tech-savvy clients, who may not represent your overall customer base.

Similarly, algorithms are designed by humans, who inevitably have biases. These biases can be mistakenly coded into these systems, resulting in distorted outcomes when they process data. Biased data can have a substantial impact on decision-making processes. They may lead to incorrect assumptions about market trends or misguided marketing plans that target non-representative customer groups.

Understanding this possible problem is critical for companies seeking clarity in their decision-making processes using DDDM methodologies, as accurate analysis is heavily reliant on unbiased data.

Cost of Data Management Infrastructure.

Setting up a strong data management infrastructure is not without financial consequences. The expense of purchasing, maintaining, and upgrading the essential gear and software can be enormous. This cost grows much larger when you include the necessity for experienced individuals to manage these systems.

However, it is critical to consider this expense as an investment rather than a cost. Investing in high-quality data management technologies can help your firm gain useful insights that push decision-making processes forward. For example, having access to real-time data may allow leaders in your firm to make timely decisions that improve business outcomes.

Furthermore, while implementing a comprehensive data management system may incur significant upfront expenses, there are possible long-term savings. Efficiently managed data eliminates redundancy and waste while increasing productivity, both of which contribute to lower operational costs over time.

To summarize, while creating a robust basis for managing organizational data requires an initial investment, the benefits of improved decision-making frequently outweigh these early costs over time.

Ethical Considerations for Data Usage

When discussing data-driven decision-making, it's crucial to note that not everything is technical or financial. When using data to make business decisions, ethical problems arise. First and foremost, businesses must be open about how they gather and use data. This transparency is critical for building confidence with customers and stakeholders. Misuse of personal information might result in a loss of credibility and possible legal consequences.

Second, there's the issue of justice. The algorithms used to analyze data should be built so that they do not favor one group over another or reinforce preexisting biases. For example, if a recruiting algorithm consistently disadvantages particular groups based on race or gender, this would be unethical behavior.

Finally, consider the problem of consent. Before collecting personal information from individuals, organizations must first obtain their explicit permission. Respect for individual privacy rights is unavoidable and is the foundation of ethical data usage.

Understanding these ethical factors allows us to ensure that our decision intelligence is respectful of persons whose information we're using while also complying with applicable laws and regulations.

Obtaining real-time insights

The capacity to process data in real time provides a substantial benefit to enterprises. It enables decision-makers to respond rapidly and effectively to changing conditions. However, reaching this level of responsiveness might be difficult.

Real-time insights necessitate powerful

technology capable of gathering, processing, and analyzing massive amounts of data extremely instantly. Not many organizations have access to these technologies or the technical competence required to effectively utilize them.

Furthermore, practical issues may occur when attempting to apply real-time analytics across multiple departments or locations within a business. Ensuring that everyone has access to the most up-to-date information at the same time might be tough, but it is critical for making consistent decisions. Despite these challenges, investing in modern data analytics technologies and techniques that allow for real-time insights can significantly increase an organization's agility and competitiveness in today's fast-paced business climate.

Benefits of Data-Driven Decision Making:

After examining the problems, let us turn our attention to the positive aspects of data-driven decision-making. When properly applied, it has the potential to alter your business operations and outcomes. Organizations that use data in decision-making processes might gain significant insights that lead to more informed and productive judgments.

This strategy has various advantages, which we shall explain in depth in this section. These include increasing operational efficiency through precision and speed, boosting strategic planning with predictive insights, personalizing customer experiences by harnessing consumer data, and driving innovation with data-driven product development strategies, among other things.

Understanding these benefits properly will prepare you to overcome any potential roadblocks on your way to becoming a genuinely data-driven corporation. So, for a more in-depth understanding, let's look at each benefit individually.

Improving operational efficiency through precision and speed.

Data-driven decision-making can dramatically increase operational efficiency. Organizations can make more precise and timely decisions when they use data. The implementation of a strong data analytics platform enables quick examination of massive amounts of information, resulting in faster insights.

For example, a firm may utilize sales data to find patterns in consumer behavior. This could result in modifications to marketing strategies or product offers that better-fit client wants, all made possible by the rapid processing and analysis of pertinent data.

The benefits are not only theoretical. Highly data-driven firms are 300% more likely to report major decision-making gains. This demonstrates that using exact, up-to-date information results in more efficient activities.

However, leaders must not only prioritize speed but also guarantee that their decisions are accurate and based on credible data. That way, individuals may be confident that their decisions will result in great outcomes rather than incurring unnecessary issues later on.

Enhancing Strategic Planning Using Predictive Insights

Strategic planning is an important aspect of any business. It is the road map that directs an organization toward its objectives. Data-driven decision-making can considerably improve the process by offering predicted insights.

Predictive analytics forecasts future events by analyzing historical data. By evaluating previous trends and patterns, we may create accurate predictions about what will happen next in our corporate environment. This foresight enables us to anticipate prospective possibilities and difficulties, resulting in more informed and successful strategic decisions.

For example, if data shows a constant increase in demand for a specific product during certain months, businesses might adjust their production schedules to meet this anticipated demand. Similarly, if consumer feedback data reveals discontent with certain components of a service, businesses can devise strategies to address these areas before they harm their reputation or bottom line. Data also allows firms to test numerous scenarios and forecast their effects without taking actual risks, such as experimenting with new marketing methods on paper before adopting them in reality.

This forward-thinking strategy would not be feasible without data-driven decision-making. Companies are more prepared than ever before to navigate uncertainty and steer toward success by embracing predictive insights drawn from trusted data sources. Remember that the goal is not only to collect data but also to properly use it - translating raw information into actionable insights that propel strategic planning processes forward.

Improving Risk Management with Data-Driven Forecasts

Risk management is an important part of any organization. The capacity to foresee and minimize prospective risks can help a company avoid major financial and reputational damages. This is where data-driven decision-making excels.

Data delivers useful insights that help firms anticipate potential risks before they arise.

Analyzing past data reveals trends that signal probable future mistakes or risks. Predictive analytics provide a safety net for decision-makers, allowing them to take proactive steps to mitigate recognized risks. For example, if sales data shows a continuous reduction in revenue during specific months of the year, businesses might prepare by modifying budget predictions or increasing marketing efforts during these times. Similarly, customer feedback data may disclose product faults that, if not handled swiftly, could result in recalls or unfavorable press. However, exploiting this level of foresight necessitates an analytical attitude among both executives and staff. Training employees on how to analyze and implement data results is critical for developing effective risk management strategies. In summary, adopting forecasts based on facts rather than gut feelings leads to better-informed risk mitigation decisions, eventually preserving your company's bottom line

Conclusion

Analytical Thinking emerges as an invaluable lighthouse in a world that requires ever-increasing insight and agility. Its ability to unravel complexity, invent solutions, and promote critical thinking enables people in a variety of fields. By nurturing a curious mind, attention to detail, and reasoning, we can go on a road of continual progress.

www.ingramcontent.com/pod-product-compliance
Lightning Source LLC
Chambersburg PA
CBHW070415230526
45471CB00006B/2816